D1171424

BULL SHARKS

The Amazing World of Sharks

BULL SHARKS

By Elizabeth Roseborough

MASON CREST

Mason Crest
450 Parkway Drive, Suite D
Broomall, Pennsylvania 19008
(866) MCP-BOOK (toll-free)
www.masoncrest.com

First printing
9 8 7 6 5 4 3 2 1
Printed in the USA

ISBN (hardback) 978-1-4222-4123-3
ISBN (series) 978-1-4222-4121-9
ISBN (ebook) 978-1-4222-7672-3

Library of Congress Cataloging-in-Publication Data

Names: Roseborough, Elizabeth, author.
Title: Bull sharks / Elizabeth Roseborough.
Description: Broomall, Pennsylvania: Mason Crest, [2019] | Series: The amazing world of sharks | Includes bibliographical references and index.
Identifiers: LCCN 2018013886 (print) | LCCN 2018018836 (ebook) | ISBN 9781422276723 (eBook) | ISBN 9781422241233 (hardback) | ISBN 9781422241219 (series)
Subjects: LCSH: Bull shark--Juvenile literature.
Classification: LCC QL638.95.C3 (ebook) | LCC QL638.95.C3 R68 2019 (print) | DDC 597.3/4--dc23
LC record available at https://lccn.loc.gov/2018013886

NATIONAL
HIGHLIGHTS

Developed and Produced by National Highlights Inc.
Editors: Keri De Deo and Mika Jin
Interior and cover design: Priceless Digital Media
Production: Michelle Luke

CONTENTS

KEY ICONS TO LOOK FOR:

 Words to Understand: These words with their easy-to-understand definitions will increase the reader's understanding of the text while building vocabulary skills.

 Sidebars: This boxed material within the main text allows readers to build knowledge, gain insights, explore possibilities, and broaden their perspectives by weaving together additional information to provide realistic and holistic perspectives.

 Educational Videos: Readers can view videos by scanning our QR codes, providing them with additional educational content to supplement the text. Examples include news coverage, moments in history, speeches, iconic sports moments, and much more!

 Text-Dependent Questions: These questions send the reader back to the text for more careful attention to the evidence presented there.

 Research Projects: Readers are pointed toward areas of further inquiry connected to each chapter. Suggestions are provided for projects that encourage deeper research and analysis.

 Series Glossary of Key Terms: This back-of-the book glossary contains terminology used throughout this series. Words found here increase the reader's ability to read and comprehend higher-level books and articles in this field.

FUN FACTS...
GETTING TO KNOW THEM

TIGER SHARK
Named for the vertical striped markings along its body, but they fade with age.

MAKO SHARK
Known as the race car of sharks for its fast swimming speed!

BULL SHARK
Named for its stocky shape, broad, flat snout, and aggressive, unpredictable behavior!

RAYS
Rays and sharks belong to the same family. A ray is basically a flattened shark.

GREAT WHITE SHARK
With jaws this fierce, they don't call it "Great" for nothing!

BLUE SHARK
Known by their distinct blue and white coloring, their large eyes, and long snout.

HAMMERHEAD SHARK
Yes, those are eyes mounted on the side of its head, giving it 360-degree vision!

THRESHER SHARK
This clever shark uses its unique long tail fin to stun and catch prey!

WORDS TO UNDERSTAND:

marine biologist: A scientist who studies animals and plants that live in salt water.
pup: A baby shark.
turbid: Water that moves rapidly and in many directions, such as the water of a bay or estuary.

CHAPTER 1

INTRODUCING BULL SHARKS

Imagine swimming at the edge of a river and seeing a gray fin pop up out of the water—it's a bull shark! While unusual, this does happen in certain large freshwater streams and rivers. Bull sharks are large, aggressive sharks that are known for swimming up freshwater rivers and streams that are connected to the ocean. While not as well known as their great white cousins, bull sharks are some of the most ferocious underwater predators in existence today. Sharks have been around since dinosaur times, and bull sharks have evolved to become incredibly good at adapting to the environment around them.

It's hard to imagine seeing a shark fin in a lake or river, but it does happen.

HOW DID BULL SHARKS GET THEIR NAME?

Bull sharks got their name for two reasons. With their aggressive nature, you might think that they got the name from their tendency to "bully," or attack other animals, but this is not the case. First, their short, blunt snout is like that of a bull's flat face. Secondly, their combative, quick-to-fight nature is like that of an aggressive bull as well. In some areas of the world, bull sharks have different names. In Africa, bull sharks are known as the Zambezi or Zambi shark. In Nicaragua, bull sharks are known as the Lake Nicaragua shark.

Bull sharks are excellent hunters and have even been known to attack land animals that wade in shallow water. They have attacked and killed dogs and sea birds—even hippopotamuses! Bull sharks are opportunistic eaters, which means that they eat whenever the opportunity presents itself. When bull sharks are hungry, they will attack anything that gets in their path, regardless of whether or not it's part of their typical diet of bony fish. It's hard to say if bull sharks attack people on purpose. It seems that humans are not the preferred food of bull sharks, but if they are hungry, they will eat whatever they can find.

Bull sharks are very diverse and can survive in both salt and fresh water.

Bull sharks are known for their violent, aggressive nature. They're likely to attack anything (or anyone) that they see as a potential threat to their territory. Without fantastic eyesight, bull sharks do not always know what they're feeling threatened by, and they find out by taking a bite! Many **marine biologists** believe that bull sharks are the most dangerous sharks in the world. Bull sharks are the sharks most likely to attack humans, followed closely by the great white shark and the tiger shark. While many shark attacks are attributed to the bull shark, it's likely that the number of attacks each year is even higher than what is reported, as it's probable that other animals are blamed for bull shark attacks, mostly because bull sharks lack distinguishing features.

Bull sharks are one of the most aggressive sharks around.

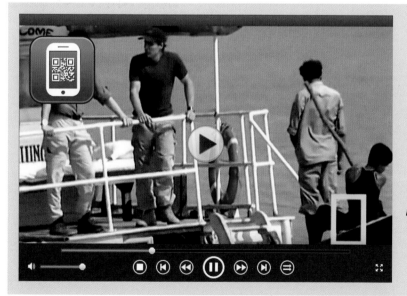

Watch this video of researchers studying shark attacks in the Bay of Bengal.

DO BULL SHARKS ATTACK HUMANS OFTEN?

While humans are not a part of the bull shark's typical diet, they will not hesitate to attack if they feel that they (or the environment in which they will give birth to their pups) are being threatened. Since bull sharks swim near coastlines, they do encounter people more often than other types of sharks would encounter people. Bull sharks are most likely to attack humans in **turbid** waters, as they may become disoriented and mistake humans for an animal that they enjoy eating. Bull sharks have also been known to attack simply out of curiosity. Often, bull sharks will do a test bite when attacking to see if the prey is something they'd be interested in eating. It's rare that they return for a second bite after taking a taste of humans.

According to the International Shark Attack File, bull sharks have been responsible for at least sixty-nine shark attacks around the world, and seventeen of those shark attacks resulted in death. It's likely that bull sharks are responsible for even more attacks than those reported. Since many shark attacks happen in murky waters, it's sometimes difficult for attack victims to describe the type of shark that bit them. The bull shark's tendency to swim in shallow waters, along with its aggressive nature, make it probable that bull sharks are responsible for the vast majority of shark attacks that happen along coastlines. The only way to truly tell whether a bite came from a great white shark or a bull shark is to examine the bite marks. Bull sharks and great whites have similar but slightly different teeth, and the shape of the bite often makes it possible to figure out which shark was responsible for the attack.

Bull sharks will wait at the river mouth for fish to swim out to sea.

SIDEBAR

Bull sharks are also known for their unusual ability to survive in both fresh and salt water. One of the things that makes bull sharks especially terrifying is their tendency to swim up large rivers that run through highly populated areas, such as the Amazon and the Mississippi. In the United States, bull sharks have been found as far inland as Indiana—a landlocked state in the middle of the country.

Bull sharks have been known to travel as far inland as Indiana.

Bull sharks have been known to travel hundreds of miles up rivers, both to hunt and to have **pups**. It's difficult to know exactly how many bull sharks travel and reside in rivers, as they prefer murky water which makes them difficult to observe. Scientists are also just beginning to learn more about bull sharks and their habits through shark tagging. While it's scary to think of a shark in a river, very few human-bull shark interactions have been recorded in fresh water. Most bull shark bites occur in shallow ocean waters. It's hard to say whether this is because bull sharks are less likely to attack in fresh water or because people are more likely to swim in shallow ocean waters than in shallow river waters. Since bull sharks give birth in fresh water, it's likely that many bull sharks in rivers and streams are young.

It's believed that most bull sharks found in rivers are quite young.

Although bull sharks are quite aggressive, they will not hunt humans out of revenge.

SHARK MYTH: SHARKS ATTACK PEOPLE WHO HAVE WRONGED THEM.

Contrary to what books and movies may lead you to believe, sharks do not go after people out of revenge. Many shark-themed movies have a storyline of sharks attacking as revenge for humans killing another shark, but this type of behavior has never been recorded. It's unlikely that sharks are capable of this level of thinking. Even if sharks were capable of feeling the need for revenge, they would not have a way of knowing which humans to attack. We do know that sharks are quite intelligent and capable of learning, however. For example, when divers regularly visit the same area with food, sharks learn that food will be available when divers arrive. While this is certainly a sign of the intelligence of sharks, this behavior is a far cry from sharks going after people because they are angry.

Bull sharks are stout and sturdy—they weigh as much as a piano and are significantly larger than the average person. Their blunt snouts and muscular bodies give them an appearance that some have likened to a bull. The bull shark's very small eyes lead some marine biologists to believe that they are unable to see well, and must rely on other senses to hunt. Since they spend much of their time in murky, muddy waters near coastlines, excellent vision would not be much of an asset anyway. Bull sharks must rely on their excellent sense of smell and their ability to sense electrical currents to find their prey.

Can you imagine a shark as big as a piano?

 TEXT-DEPENDENT QUESTIONS:

1. Where do most bull shark attacks occur?

2. Name one feature of bull sharks that is different from most sharks.

3. What's another name that the bull shark is called?

 RESEARCH PROJECT:

Bull sharks are one of the ocean animals that are most feared by swimmers and divers. Research three bull shark attacks that have happened in the last century.

WORDS TO UNDERSTAND:

brackish: Water that is a mixture of fresh and salt water, such as that found in a bay or estuary.

ecosystem: A community of interacting living things and their physical environment, such as the ocean.

euryhaline: An animal that is able to tolerate wide variations in the amount of salt in their underwater habitat.

extinct: A species of plant or animal of which there are no living members.

subtropical: Areas outside of the equator that tend to have warm, humid climates. Subtropical areas are not as warm as tropical areas.

CHAPTER 2

THE BULL SHARK'S POPULATION AND HABITAT

POPULATION

Scientists are working hard to track bull sharks to learn how many of them exist in the wild, but right now, there is not enough data to know exactly how many bull sharks are currently living. That being said, marine biologists hypothesize that the bull shark population is declining, as bull sharks are regularly being killed due to human-created issues such as bycatch and beach protection programs. Being apex predators, it is unlikely that the bull shark's population decline is due to overhunting from other animals.

It is believed that the bull shark's decline is due to overfishing by humans.

Tracking bull sharks can be difficult and dangerous due to their violent, aggressive nature, but it's important to track them to learn more about their population, hunting habits, and migration. There are a few different ways that marine biologists are currently tracking sharks.

In order to tag a shark, the shark must first be caught, brought onto a boat, and sedated by scientists. Usually, this requires marine biologists to go to an area known for sharks and then chum the waters to attract sharks to the boat. Chumming the waters is a process in which buckets containing blood and pieces of fish are tossed overboard in an effort to attract sharks. After the shark is caught, a large sling is suspended from the boat. The sling goes underneath the shark's body and is used to lift them on board the boat. At this point, the shark is sedated, so that it does not begin to feel threatened and attack the people on board. The tag is then attached to the shark's dorsal fin, where it remains for the rest of the shark's life.

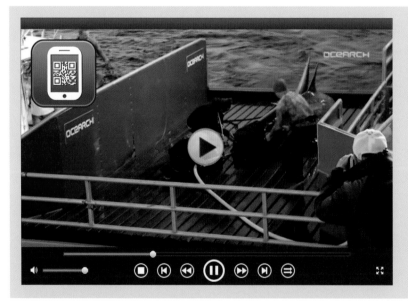

Although not a bull shark, this video demonstrates how sharks are captured and tagged by marine biologists.

While this tagging does cause momentary bleeding and discomfort for the shark, it is essential that scientists learn more about the habits of sharks so that they are able to protect them from further population decline. The momentary discomfort is a small trade-off for all of the information that scientists are able to learn from the data gathered by the tag. After the tag is attached to the dorsal fin, the shark is released back to the ocean. While sharks do initially swim more slowly when they are returned to the ocean, within two to four hours, they are back to swimming normally. As sharks swim, their dorsal fin often breaks the surface of the water. Each time this happens, the tag sends a "ping" to a science lab. The scientists working in these labs use the pings to create maps that show where the shark has traveled. This data is used to learn more about where sharks swim, hunt, mate, and give birth. They migrate, have babies, and hunt the same way as an untagged shark. Studies have shown that the tagging process does not cause any long-term damage to the shark's fin.

When a shark is tagged, the hope is that the tag stays on for the entirety of the shark's life, providing years of valuable information about the shark's movement patterns. Shark tags are expensive, and it can take a lot of time for scientists to attract and catch a shark. Sometimes, the tags become

Untagged sharks and tagged sharks swim and act the same.

damaged or come loose from the shark's fin. When a tag is lost or damaged, it becomes impossible to know whether the shark was killed or if the tag simply stopped functioning. Marine biologists are constantly researching the best way to tag sharks.

CONSERVATION STATUS

Bull sharks are currently listed as near threatened by the International Union for Conservation of Nature and Natural Resources (IUCN). The IUCN is the organization that determines the conservation levels for all animals, from least concern up to **extinct**, based upon whether an animal's population is increasing or decreasing. The near-threatened level is second from the bottom of the list (the bottom of the list is least concern). The bull shark's near-threatened status means that if current environmental and man-made threats against bull sharks continue, they're likely to become endangered, and possibly extinct. While it may seem like there is plenty of time to begin conservation efforts, it's important to start sooner rather than later.

Since bull sharks are often spotted along coastlines, it's easy to assume that there are lots of them. Near threatened does not mean that there are only a few bull sharks in the wild. It means that their population is

going down at a steady rate, and that protective measures need to be taken to ensure that their population can stabilize or increase. Scientists are working hard to learn exactly how many bull sharks remain in the wild so that they can take action to ensure the survival of their population.

Bull sharks are considered near threatened and action is needed to save them.

THREATS TO POPULATION

Bycatch

Unlike many other types of sharks, bull sharks are not regularly hunted for sport or for meat, but this does not mean that bull sharks are safe from humans. Commercial fishermen sometimes catch them accidentally. Often, when fishermen are attempting to catch other ocean animals (such as tuna), bull sharks get tangled in the nets that are being used to catch the other fish. This causes a few issues. If bull sharks remain entangled in the net and get on board the ship, they are often killed due to the danger they pose to the people on board. Commercial fishermen usually do not attempt to sedate the shark and return it to the water, as this would increase the cost of commercial fishing and create a greater danger for those on board. It's difficult to get close enough to the shark to push it overboard without getting injured. If a bull shark is entangled in the net and manages to escape, it is often left with injuries that eventually lead to its death.

Bull sharks can get caught in fishermen's nets accidentally. This often leads to the shark's death.

BEACH PROTECTION PROGRAMS

South Africa and Australia both have bull shark beach protection programs designed to keep swimmers and surfers safe from shark attacks. Nets are strung up in the coastal waters near beaches with the intention of catching bull sharks so that they can be released to an area in which they will be less likely to encounter humans. While these nets do work to catch

Shark nets, such as this one in Australia, are often used to keep sharks away from swimmers.

sharks, the sharks are often injured, either while trapped in the net or during the release process. Many sharks die while trapped in the nets. These nets are dangerous to all sharks, but especially to bull sharks that tend to swim in coastal areas.

JAWS: THE MATAWAN CREEK ATTACKS

In 1916, five people died from shark attacks in New Jersey over a twelve-day period. These attacks were the inspiration for the movie *Jaws*. Three of the attacks happened in the Matawan Creek. It's unlikely that these swimmers were aware that sharks were even a possibility in the creek, as it is more than 15 miles (24 km) from the open ocean. A few days later, both a bull shark and a great white shark were found a few miles from the creek's opening. The great white shark's stomach contained human remains, but many theorized that the aggressive bull shark was responsible for at least some of the attacks. There has been much controversy over the years as to which shark was to blame for the attacks.

This newspaper clippings demonstrates how sharks were viewed in 1916.

WHY SHARKS MATTER AND HOW TO HELP

Many people have the untrue belief that the fewer sharks that are in the ocean, the better, but nothing could be further from the truth. All sharks are an important part of the ocean's healthy **ecosystem**. Sharks are apex predators, which means that generally, they are at the top of the food chain. They are predators, but adult sharks are rarely (except in special cases) prey. This is important because the predatory habits of sharks help keep other populations in check. Sharks also tend to prey on weak and sick members of other populations, which can stop disease from spreading.

Without sharks, other populations in the ocean would grow out of control, and eventually, there would not be enough food for all the members of these populations to survive. A healthy ecosystem needs balance from top to bottom, and that means that apex predators are helping, not hurting, the ocean.

Animals that sharks prey on often learn where the sharks tend to go when they're looking for food. In time, the preyed-upon species realizes that it's a good idea to stay away from these areas. This regular movement of animal populations helps protect coral reefs and sea grass. When animal populations grow out of control, animals that eat coral and sea grass may destroy it to the point that it is unable to regrow.

Sharks help keep fish populations down, which helps protect coral reefs like this one in Indonesia.

When sharks are removed from coral reef ecosystems, the fish that they typically prey on increase drastically. Many of the fish that sharks prey on are large predatory fish. These large predatory fish typically prey on herbivore (plant-eating) fish, and when there are too many large predatory fish, the population of herbivore fish decreases. Without herbivores, the algae in coral reefs begins to grow out of control, causing damage or death to the reef. Coral reefs are home to a wide variety of marine plant and animal life, and their destruction can result in extinction or endangerment of a wide variety of species.

Sharks are also important to the fishing industry. Studies have shown that when sharks are removed from an area, ray populations can grow out of control, as sharks often prey on rays. In one particular study, the ray population grew so out of control that they eliminated their favorite food—scallops—from the North Carolina coastal area, causing a fishery to close.

Sharks help keep the population of rays at a healthy level so they do not destroy the ecosystem.

Sharks are also an important part of the economy in many coastal locations that are popular vacation destinations. Shark diving businesses depend on a large shark population to keep scuba divers coming back. When shark populations dwindle, shark diving businesses are not able to provide diving trips.

Clearly, sharks are important to both the ocean and the humans that live on the surrounding coasts. Many people do not understand that sharks are important—they simply see them as a dangerous predator that should be eliminated. Some people even hold the untrue belief that the only good shark is a dead shark. One way to help keep sharks safe is simply to educate others about why sharks are so important to the ocean. A way to do this is to talk with your science teacher about giving a presentation to your class about the importance of sharks. Talking about why apex predators are a vital part of the ocean's health can help others understand why sharks are such a key component of the food chain.

Another way to help shark populations increase is to write to the lawmakers at the beach closest to you about the importance of sharks, and encourage them to pass laws that protect sharks. Currently, there are no laws in place anywhere in the world to protect bull sharks from harm. There are laws in place to protect other sharks, and it's important that similar laws be enacted to protect bull sharks. Since bull sharks are in near-threatened status, it is essential to their survival as a species that protective measures be put in place by lawmakers.

When you purchase seafood, it's important to be aware of the fishing practices of the seafood company. Some fishing companies have more issues with bycatch than others, and there are certain fishing companies that engage in special fishing practices that allow them to reduce the amount of harm done to other sea creatures, such as dolphins, sea turtles, and sharks. In the internet resources section of this book, you'll find a website that will help you determine which seafood companies use responsible fishing practices that reduce or eliminate bycatch issues.

Watch this video to see how some scientists are using technology to get close to sharks.

When you go on vacation, it's crucial that you don't purchase souvenirs that were once a part of a shark's body, such as teeth or jaws. It's likely that these souvenirs are not real. If they are real, it's probable that the shark was killed for a part of its body.

As mentioned, it's expensive for marine biologists to learn more about sharks, but learning more is the only way to help keep sharks safe and begin to increase their populations. Giving money to organizations that protect animals, such as the World Wildlife Foundation (WWF), is a great way to contribute to helping scientists research sharks. To make an even bigger impact, you can ask for a donation to the WWF in your name for your birthday or Christmas.

HABITAT

Bull sharks are found all over the world in tropical and **subtropical** waters. Most species of sharks are only able to swim in salt water, but bull sharks have the ability to swim in both fresh and salt water. As **euryhaline** animals, bull sharks can move freely between the two types of water, as their bodies are able to automatically adjust. Bull sharks spend most of their time in the ocean,

BULL SHARKS IN THE AMAZON

The Amazon River is an incredibly large river that runs nearly the entire width of South America. Bull sharks are known for swimming far into the Amazon. The furthest reported catch of a bull shark in the Amazon River was 2,485 miles (4,000 km) inland from the Atlantic Ocean! The bull shark's strong fins allow it to fight currents, swimming far upriver.

but have also been known to spend time in **brackish** water, as well as swim hundreds of miles up rivers to hunt and have babies. Bull sharks prefer to swim in shallow ocean waters and are often observed hunting along shallow tropical shorelines. Bull sharks are capable of swimming in depths of up to 490 ft. (150 m), but are rarely observed swimming in waters deeper than 98 ft. (30 m).

In the Indian Ocean, bull sharks are found from the Philippines to Australia, from Kenya to South Africa, as well as in the coastal waters of Vietnam and India. In the Atlantic Ocean, bull sharks are found from the shorelines of the northeastern United States down to the coast of Brazil, and from the shores of Angola up to the coast of Morocco.

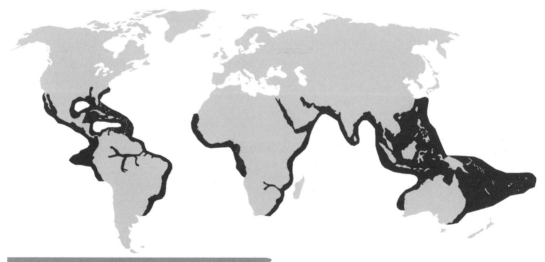

This map demonstrates the bull shark's distribution across the globe.

MIGRATION

While bull sharks prefer to stay in warm waters no matter what the time of year, they do show some predictable migration based on the season. Many bull sharks migrate to the Caribbean during the winter months, and return to the coastal waters of the northeastern United States when the water becomes warm in the summer.

In addition to seasonal migration, bull sharks also migrate in order to reproduce. Bull sharks are often found in the Gulf of Mexico during late spring and early summer to find a mate. After mating, most bull sharks leave the area. Female bull sharks wait ten to eleven months until their pups are ready to be born. When it's time to give birth, female bull sharks travel inland to freshwater rivers and streams. Pups tend to spend a significant amount of time in fresh water before traveling out to salt water. Most marine biologists agree that mother bull sharks choose to give birth in fresh water because there are fewer predators there than in the open ocean. Bull shark pups are often hunted by other animals, including older bull sharks, when they are in the open ocean.

TEXT-DEPENDENT QUESTIONS:

1. What is the bull shark's conservation status?

2. How are beach protection programs harmful to bull sharks?

3. Why are apex predators an important part of the ocean's ecosystem?

RESEARCH PROJECT:

Many bull sharks have been observed swimming in a golf course lake in Brisbane, Australia, which is a completely landlocked body of water. Research how the sharks got there and how they continue to survive.

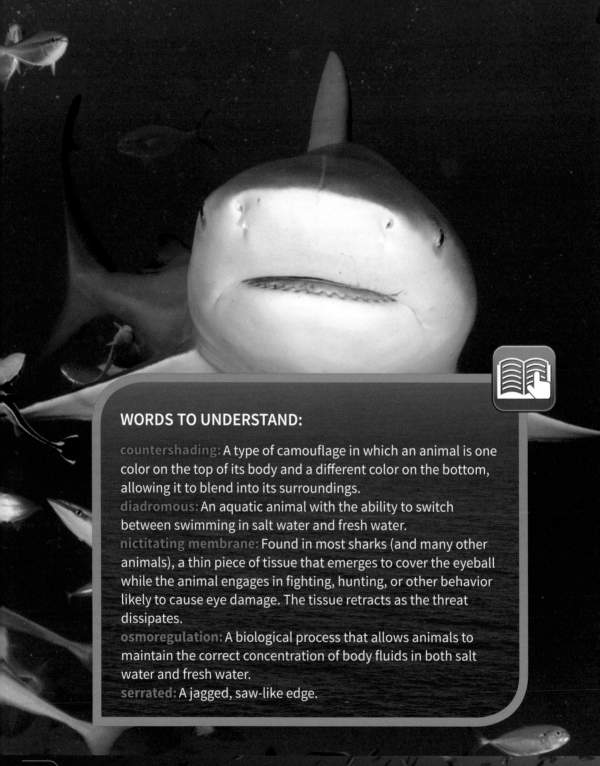

WORDS TO UNDERSTAND:

countershading: A type of camouflage in which an animal is one color on the top of its body and a different color on the bottom, allowing it to blend into its surroundings.

diadromous: An aquatic animal with the ability to switch between swimming in salt water and fresh water.

nictitating membrane: Found in most sharks (and many other animals), a thin piece of tissue that emerges to cover the eyeball while the animal engages in fighting, hunting, or other behavior likely to cause eye damage. The tissue retracts as the threat dissipates.

osmoregulation: A biological process that allows animals to maintain the correct concentration of body fluids in both salt water and fresh water.

serrated: A jagged, saw-like edge.

CHAPTER 3

THE BULL SHARK'S DIET, BEHAVIOR, AND BIOLOGY

DIET

The bull shark's diet consists mostly of bony fish such as tarpon, catfish, snook, mackerel, and fish that travel in schools. When fish are scarce, bull sharks will eat dolphins, sea turtles, and even other sharks (including pups of their own species). When a bull shark is hungry, it will eat literally anything—including sea trash. Bull sharks do not have a preference for hunting during the day or at night; they will hunt whenever food is available, as they are opportunistic eaters.

Bull sharks are opportunistic eaters, meaning they'll eat what they can find.

Bull sharks are known for attacking land animals, including cows, hippopotamuses, dogs, and sea birds, that venture into shallow coastal waters. When waiting to attack a land animal, bull sharks stay very still in the water, as it's important that their prey does not notice the movement of the bull shark's gray fin that typically pokes out of the water's surface. It's easy to assume that bull sharks are sluggish due to their large size, but they are actually able to swim at speeds up to 11 mph (19 kmph), making it difficult for any prey to run or swim away. Although this speed might sound slow, it's important to remember that land animals move much more slowly in water than they do on land, giving bull sharks a speed advantage.

BEHAVIOR

Bull sharks are known for being extremely territorial and aggressive. They are very fast swimmers, and they give little warning before they attack (both while hunting and while defending their territory). Their behavior is unpredictable. Young bull sharks have been observed breaching the water, but this behavior has never been observed in older bull sharks.

Other than during mating season, bull sharks usually prefer to swim alone. There have been a few atypical cases of bull sharks swimming in pairs— the reason for this behavior is unclear. Mating occurs in spring and summer. Often, bull sharks travel to the waters of the Gulf of Mexico for mating season, and then females travel to fresh or brackish waters to have their pups.

Bull sharks have been seen in groups, but they prefer to be alone most of the time.

HUNTING

Known for hunting in shallow coastal waters, bull sharks are efficient hunters. Bull sharks have a unique hunting technique. They often head-butt their prey before attacking, delivering a confusing stun to their next meal. Their snouts are wider than they are long, which allows them to perform the equivalent of hitting their prey over the head with a brick. This disorients their prey and often helps bull sharks make a quick and easy kill.

PREDATOR *AND* PREY?

The bull shark is one of the most ferocious predators known to man, but at times, these dangerous sea creatures also become prey. Young bull sharks grow very slowly and can fall prey to adult bull sharks, tiger sharks, and sandbar sharks. There have also been unconfirmed reports of saltwater crocodiles attacking and killing bull sharks. Large predators tend to stay away from flat areas, which explains why it's helpful for young bull sharks to spend their time in fresh water (freshwater areas tend to be flatter than the floor of the ocean). It is extremely rare that an adult bull shark would be attacked unless it is sick or weak and another predator believes that the bull shark will be an easy kill.

Check out this video to see how marine biologists are studying the hunting habits of bull sharks.

BIOLOGY

Size

Bull sharks range from 200 to 500 lbs. (91 to 267 kg), and range from 7 to 11.5 ft. (2.1 to 3.5 m) in length, and females tend to be larger than males. Compared to other sharks, bull sharks are neither large nor small. They have long pectoral fins that help them swim quickly and gracefully. The tips of their pectoral fins can be dark. Often, the pectoral fin tips are darkest when the bull sharks are pups, and they fade to blend in with the rest of the pectoral fin as the sharks age.

Bull sharks are large and bulky animals, but they're fast swimmers.

DISTINGUISHING FEATURES

The bull shark has a wide snout and small eyes. Its snout is much wider than it is long, giving it a rectangular appearance. Like most sharks, a bull shark's eyes contain a **nictitating membrane**, which comes out from behind the eye socket, keeping its eyes safe from harm during fighting and hunting. A bull shark's strong jaw gives it the most powerful

Bull sharks have small eyes and triangular teeth.

bite of any shark in the ocean with the ability to chomp with 1,300 lbs. (592 kg) of force. A force this strong makes it easy for bull sharks to break shells and bone with a single bite. Their incredible jaws are filled with hundreds of very sharp teeth. Their teeth are in rows that are able to rotate as necessary. The first two rows are used to catch prey, and the other rows rotate in as necessary when teeth are lost or broken. This works like a conveyer belt—when a tooth is lost, the next tooth in line moves up into its place. Their teeth are **serrated** and triangular, allowing for easy biting and tearing of prey.

Bull sharks have two dorsal (top) fins: the first significantly larger than the second. Both dorsal fins come to a point. They have two pectoral fins that they use like arms to swim quickly through the water. Their pectoral fins are large and angled down from their bodies. Bull sharks have large tails, also known as caudal fins. The dorsal half of the caudal fin is larger than the ventral (lower) half. A large caudal fin allows the bull shark to build speed quickly when hunting. Bull sharks use their caudal fin to maneuver easily around their prey. This is especially important when hunting fish that travel in schools. The bull shark's quick, agile movements serve to confuse its prey.

Like all sharks, bull sharks have a collection of small organs called the ampullae of Lorenzini. These small receptors near the shark's snout allow it to sense electrical signals that travel through the water. While these ampullae take the form of small, jelly-filled pores and look much different than other sensory organs, they are just as valuable as eyes, ears, or a nose. All animals emit electrical signals, and bull sharks are able to use these electrical signals to learn more about the location and type of prey available to them. Being able to sense these signals and use them to find prey is a sense that humans do not have—it's called electroreception.

Bull sharks look similar to other sharks, but there are some differences.

A healthy animal emits a different signal than an animal that is sick or in distress. When sharks sense that an animal is in distress, they often follow the electrical signal and then go in for the easy kill. Being able to rely on electricity to hunt is important when bull sharks are looking for food at night, or when they are swimming through murky waters. While the ampullae of Lorenzini are important for hunting, many marine biologists believe that sharks also use their electroreception for travel. The earth emits small electrical signals. When these signals travel through water, sharks are able to pick up on them. It's possible that sharks use a combination of these electrical signals and the ocean's tides like a road map, guiding them on their journeys.

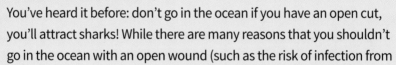

SHARKS AND BLOOD

You've heard it before: don't go in the ocean if you have an open cut, you'll attract sharks! While there are many reasons that you shouldn't go in the ocean with an open wound (such as the risk of infection from bacteria in the water), the likelihood that you'll attract a shark due to a cut is quite low. Many people believe that sharks can smell blood from miles away, making swimmers, surfers, and divers susceptible to shark attacks if they enter the ocean with a small cut. It's understandable why some people would think this, as most sharks do have very sensitive noses. Some can even smell blood at one part per billion. While that is an impressive sense of smell compared to most animals, the ocean is vast. Even smelling blood at one part per ten billion is comparable to a shark being able to find blood (or bleeding prey) in an area the size of an Olympic swimming pool. If a shark is not already in the general vicinity of blood, it will not be aware of its presence. A shark's nostrils are found on the underside of its snout, and their sole purpose is to smell—they aren't used for breathing, since sharks do not breathe air. Water flows into the shark's nostrils, brushing against tissue that sends signals to the shark's brain about the scents in the water. When it comes to a shark detecting prey by smell, there are a variety of factors to consider—ocean current, age of the shark, whether or not the prey is injured, and other substances in the water, just to name a few. While it's unlikely that you'd attract a shark if you get a cut in the ocean, it's still a good idea to get out of the water and get it cleaned up before you go back to swimming.

REPRODUCTION

Most sharks lay eggs, but bull sharks are a little bit different. Bull shark mothers give birth to live shark pups, no eggshell involved. There are very few non-mammalian animals that give birth to live young. Pregnant bull shark moms typically give birth to one to three pups at a time. Male bull sharks have the ability to reproduce from the time they are between fourteen and fifteen years old, but female bull sharks do not have the ability to reproduce until they reach eighteen years old.

When it's time to give birth, pregnant bull sharks travel to fresh or brackish waters, as these areas are shallow and offer the pups more protection from predators than the open ocean. When bull shark pups are born, they are able to swim and hunt on their own. The mother shark does not stick around to protect her offspring. Bull shark pups are on their own from the time that they are born, which leaves them susceptible to many predators. Many of the largest aquatic predators cannot survive in fresh water, so shark pups stay safe by staying in fresh water for anywhere from a few months to a few years after they are born. The first few years of a bull shark's life can be very dangerous, as they must figure out their underwater world on their own.

FROM SALT WATER TO FRESH WATER

Bull sharks are **diadromous**, meaning they can easily switch between swimming in salt water and swimming in fresh water. Most aquatic animals do not have this ability—they can swim in salt water or fresh water, but not both. The bull shark is able to make this switch due to its unusual ability to osmoregulate. **Osmoregulation** is an internal process that allows an animal to adjust its internal body chemistry so that it is well suited for the environment outside of its body. This process is key in allowing bull sharks to move back and forth between salt water and fresh water with ease.

Bull sharks can easily adapt to salt water and fresh water.

All animals (including humans!) are made of cells with semi-permeable membranes. A semi-permeable membrane surrounds the cell to keep it safe. This membrane works like a fence. It lets some substances in and lets some substances out, depending on the needs of the animal's body. In a shark, water moves in and out of its cells, as well as in and out of its skin. When a shark is swimming in salt water, the salt moves in and out of its skin and cells along with the water. All fish (including sharks) have some salt in their bodies. In most ocean animals, their bodies will move water in and out until the level of salt inside their bodies matches the level of salt in the water around them. This explains why it's so dangerous for most marine animals to venture into fresh water. When they leave salt water and swim up a stream or river, they lose much of the valuable salt in their bodies, which can cause a chemical imbalance that can lead to sickness or death. Most ocean animals instinctively know that they must stay in salt water.

Bull sharks have kidneys that are different from those of other sharks—a bull shark's kidneys work much, much harder than the kidneys of most animals, in fact. A bull shark's kidneys allow it to osmoregulate. As fresh water or salt water moves in and out of the cells of a shark, its kidneys are constantly adjusting the level of salt in its body to the level of salt in the water around it, while keeping the concentrations of both salt and water to a level that sustains its life processes. Most sharks are not able to do this, but bull sharks (and a few other sharks, including the Ganges River shark) have this special ability that allows them to not only survive, but also thrive, in almost any aquatic environment.

A bull shark's kidneys are able to rid its body of excess salt through urination. Bull sharks have a special organ near their tails that helps them get rid of excess salt. Salt plays a very important role in the bodies of all living things, as it helps the brain transmit signals to the rest of the body to complete vital life processes, such as keeping the heart beating. While getting rid of excess salt is important, it's also imperative that bull sharks do not get rid of too much salt, as this could cause illness or death as well. These processes happen automatically—a bull shark never has to think about controlling the level of salt in its body.

A bull shark's ability to osmoregulate seems to increase with age. Young bull sharks are usually observed in the freshwater environments into which they were born, and older bull sharks are usually found in salt water, leading scientists to believe that their kidneys develop the ability to filter out large amounts of salt over time. It's hard to know how young bull sharks know when it's time to leave their freshwater environment and move to the open ocean, but it's likely an instinctual process as they do not have their mothers around to guide them.

The ability to osmoregulate gives bull sharks many advantages over animals without this ability. When a bull shark mother has her babies in fresh water, they are hidden from ocean predators. When food in the ocean becomes scarce, bull sharks are able to hunt in freshwater areas inaccessible to other ocean creatures. In cases of man-made ocean problems (construction, oil spills), bull sharks have an entirely separate habitat available to them.

COLORING

Bull sharks exhibit **countershading**, as they are gray on top and white on the bottom. Many animals have countershading, meaning that different parts of their bodies are different colors to help them blend in with their surroundings and hide from predators. Countershading is important for keeping sharks safe from harm, especially when they are young and likely to be attacked by other sharks. When viewed from above, their gray top helps them to blend in with the dark ocean floor below, keeping them hidden from human hunters. When viewed from below, their white bellies allow them to blend in with the water's surface and the sky, keeping them nearly invisible to animals (such as great white sharks, tiger sharks, and older bull sharks) who may intend to cause them harm.

LIFE SPAN

The average life span of a bull shark in the wild is sixteen years, meaning that the average female bull shark never grows old enough to reproduce. It's important to remember that this number is an average and is skewed because many bull sharks are attacked when they are pups and never make it to adulthood. Scientists estimate that bull sharks are likely to be able to live up to twenty-seven years, but due to illness, injury, and bycatch, many die in about half that time.

TEXT-DEPENDENT QUESTIONS:

1. What special organ allows sharks to sense electrical currents in the water?

2. How do bull sharks hunt?

3. Bull sharks are diadromous animals. What does that mean?

RESEARCH PROJECT:

Bull sharks are one of the few animals with the ability to osmoregulate. Many of their close relatives do not have this ability. Research how scientists believe this ability evolved over time.

WORDS TO UNDERSTAND:

captivity: A man-made, non-natural animal habitat, such as an aquarium or zoo.

retinal cone: The part of the eye that detects light.

salinity: The level of salt in water.

CHAPTER 4

ENCOUNTERING A BULL SHARK

Bull sharks are aggressive and territorial—they are not an animal that most people want to encounter while swimming! Given the fact that many marine biologists agree that bull sharks are the most dangerous animals in the ocean, it's a good idea to steer clear of these animals in the wild. For adventure seekers, it is possible to dive with bull sharks, both through cage diving and free diving. If you choose to dive with sharks, it's important that you do so with a qualified professional. Never attempt to dive with sharks on your own.

Although risky, it is possible to dive with sharks, such as this blacktip shark and the bull shark.

If you're interested in diving with sharks, whether you choose to dive in a cage or free dive, it's important to consider the time of year and the time of day. Research the time of year that sharks are most likely to be visiting the location in which you'd like to dive. In many areas, sharks are most active in the morning. The diving company you choose will be able to give you information on the best time to see sharks. Remember, although sharks do show movement patterns, they are unpredictable. Sharks can be in the water at any time, and it's important to always keep an eye out for bull sharks in shallow coastal waters.

Watch as these divers feed hungry bull sharks by hand!

SIDEBAR

CAN BULL SHARKS SURVIVE IN AQUARIUMS?

There are some aquariums that do feature bull sharks in their exhibits, but many aquariums have found that bull sharks do not survive well in **captivity**. Marine biologists are unsure why some bull sharks do well in some aquariums, and not in others. There are a number of factors that come into play when creating a healthy aquarium—water **salinity**, diet, other animals in the tank, water temperature—and it has been difficult for scientists to pin down exactly what helps bull sharks survive outside of their natural environment. There is currently a high demand for bull sharks in aquariums, as many people are fascinated with aggressive sharks. While it can be interesting to see bull sharks up close, removing them from their natural habitat can cause their population to decrease.

The man-made lagoon system for sharks in Australia makes it possible for people to see sharks up close without getting into the water with them.

CAGE DIVING WITH BULL SHARKS

Cage diving is a way to encounter sharks in their natural habitat without the danger of free diving. Cage diving is not something that you can do alone. There are many coastal areas that offer cage diving. When embarking on a cage diving trip, your boat captain will pick you up and have you board the boat. You'll be taken to a location known for bull sharks. While it's likely that sharks will be present, it's always possible that they won't come around, as their habits are unpredictable. When you get to your destination, the boat crew will talk to you about the rules of cage diving. The boat crew may chum the waters, depending on whether or not sharks are already present. Chumming the waters is a controversial practice, as many marine biologists believe that it's dangerous to teach sharks that they will get food when they see a boat.

After the boat crew sees that sharks are present, you'll be given an apparatus to breathe through, as well as a way to let the boat crew know if you need to exit the water at any time (usually a small button on your breathing apparatus). The boat crew will have you practice with the breathing apparatus to make sure you understand how to use it. Remember—it's a good idea to ask questions if anything seems confusing!

One way to see a shark is to cage dive.

When it's time for your dive, you'll enter the metal cage. The bars of the cage are spaced far enough apart that you can easily see out into the water, but close enough together that sharks are unable to enter the cage. You'll need to be careful to keep your hands and feet inside the cage, as any part of you that is out of the cage may look like a snack to a shark. The boat crew will secure the top of the cage to keep you safe. You'll then be lowered into the water. The cage will be attached to the boat with a steel chain. Once you are lowered into the water, you'll likely have the experience of getting to observe sharks (and other animals) in their natural habitat.

Sharks have their own personalities, so no two cage dives will be the same. Some sharks are interested in the cage and will want to come up close to check it out, while others will barely notice the cage is there, especially if they're interested in something more fun (like food nearby). Even though you may be excited to see a shark, it's important that you don't try to bother the shark in any way.

While cage diving is relatively safe, wild animals are unpredictable, and there is the chance of injury. If you choose to cage dive, it's important to be aware of the risks involved.

FREE DIVING WITH BULL SHARKS

For extreme thrill seekers, free diving with sharks can be exciting! While diving with sharks is usually safe when done with a trained professional, it's important to remember that sharks are wild animals, and wild animals can be unpredictable and dangerous.

Before you're able to free dive at all, you'll need to get your scuba certification. Even if you don't live in an area near the ocean, many indoor pools offer scuba certification classes. If you live in a cold area, look for an indoor pool that offers certifications. If you get your certification in a pool, it's especially important to listen to the instructions of your boat crew when free diving, as the open ocean is a very different environment than the bottom of a pool. Be sure to ask any questions that you may have, especially those pertaining to interacting with animals.

Some people want to get very close to sharks, so they scuba dive with an expert.

There are many places in North America that allow you to free dive with bull sharks, including coastal locations in Mexico and the United States. Since it's never safe to free dive alone, it's important to book a diving trip with a scuba expert. Be sure to check the boat crew's certification on their website before booking a trip. Your safety is the number one concern of the diving company, and they may have requirements beyond scuba certification. Many companies require that you are an experienced ocean diver before they will permit you to dive with sharks.

When you go free diving, your boat captain will pick you up and drive the boat to the location where you will dive with sharks. The boat crew may chum the waters to attract sharks to the area in which you will be diving. Just like with cage diving, it's important to remember that although your boat captain is taking you to an area known for sharks, it's possible that you may simply be enjoying other sea creatures, as bull sharks are unpredictable and may not return to the same location every day. While on board, your boat crew will explain the rules for the dive. It's crucial that you listen closely, as the rules will tell you how to keep yourself safe, and how to signal to the boat crew if you have a problem while diving. Most likely, some of the boat crew will dive with you. The crew may bring down additional bait to feed to sharks. While many companies do this to ensure that sharks show up during dives, some marine biologists do not think that this practice should be allowed. When sharks begin to expect food from divers, it becomes possible that they could

Playa del Carmen in Mexico is a popular place for shark diving.

be angry and aggressive if divers show up without food at another time, potentially leading to attacks. Often, sharks will simply swim around as they normally would, not paying any attention to divers.

While free diving with sharks can be dangerous, it can also be the experience of a lifetime. Just like with cage diving, it's important to be aware of the possibility of injury and attack while free diving.

SHARK ATTACK!

When cage diving and free diving, participants want to see bull sharks. Most of the time, however, a gray fin is not something you want to see while you're swimming! It's important to know what to do in the event that you are in the water and encounter a bull shark. If you're swimming in shallow coastal water and encounter a shark, the likelihood is high that it's a bull shark. As you know, bull sharks are some of the most dangerous and aggressive ocean creatures known to man, so it's imperative that you act quickly and carefully.

STAYING SAFE: HIDE IN PLAIN SIGHT

If you're swimming in an area that is known for bull sharks, it's important to do everything you can to protect yourself from a potential attack. Recent studies show that a bull shark's eyes may not be able to detect color in the same way as a human's eyes. Bull shark eyes only have one type of retinal cone. It allows them to see red and black. To compare, humans have three different types of cones to detect different colors. According to the International Shark Attack File, most bull shark attacks on divers have occurred when the divers were wearing black wet suits, making it likely that the bull shark mistook the diver for something tastier. Remember, even if you dress in bright colors, shark attacks are still possible. It's important not to get into the water if you see a shark.

Unless you're with a professional group or expert, do not go looking for sharks.

The best way to defend yourself against a shark attack is to prevent the attack from happening in the first place. Before you get into the water, take a look at your surroundings. If the water is murky and dark, it's not a good idea to get in. Bull sharks like to hunt in dark water, and if you cannot see through the water clearly, it's impossible for you to know if a shark is present. If you can see animals such as turtles or rays in the water, pay attention to their behavior. If you see them behaving erratically or swimming quickly, there's a good chance that a dangerous predator is nearby. Always go into the ocean with a friend or two. Swimming alone is dangerous because there is no one to help you if you get into trouble. If you're in the water and you feel something brush against your leg, it's important to get out and make sure that you haven't been bitten. Many shark attack victims say that they do not feel pain during the attack and do not realize that they have been bitten.

In the unlikely event that a shark attacks you, it's important that you fight as hard as you can! "Playing dead" does not cause the shark to lose interest, and is likely to do more harm than good. Hitting the shark on its sensitive

A shark's nose is often the most sensitive body part, so hitting it in case of an attack could deter the shark.

nose and eyes can deter it from continuing the attack. When you free yourself from the shark, exit the water as quickly as possible. No matter how small the bite, it's important that you report your encounter to the authorities and seek medical attention. Doing so will help to keep other swimmers safe.

 TEXT-DEPENDENT QUESTIONS:

1. What two colors are bull sharks most likely to be able to see?

2. Why is it important to note the behavior of nearby animals before you enter the water?

3. When free diving, there's no guarantee that you'll encounter a shark. Why not?

 RESEARCH PROJECT:

Research the safety of diving with sharks, including how many attacks have been reported during planned dives. Research safety measures that are taken to ensure the safety of divers.

SERIES GLOSSARY OF KEY TERMS

Apparatus: A device or a collection of tools that are used for a specific purpose. A diving apparatus helps you breathe under water.

Barbaric: Something that is considered unrefined or uncivilized. The idea of killing sharks just for their fins can be seen as barbaric.

Buoyant: Having the ability to float. Not all sharks are buoyant. They need to swim to stay afloat.

Camouflage: To conceal or hide something. Sharks' coloring often helps camouflage them from their prey.

Chum: A collection of fish guts and fish remains thrown into the ocean to attract sharks. Divers will often use chum to help attract sharks.

Conservation: The act of preserving or keeping things safe. Conservation is important in keeping sharks and oceans safe from humans.

Decline: To slope down or to decrease in number. Shark populations are on the decline due to human activity.

Delicacy: Something, particularly something to eat, that is very special and rare. Shark fin soup is seen as a delicacy in some Asian countries, but it causes a decline in shark populations.

Expedition: A type of adventure that involves travel for a specific purpose. Traveling to a location specifically to see sharks would be considered an expedition.

Ferocious: Describes something that is mean, fierce, or extreme. Sharks often look ferocious because of their teeth and the way they attack their prey.

Finning: The act of cutting off the top (dorsal) fin of a shark specifically to sell for meat. Sharks cannot swim without all of their fins, so finning leads to a shark's death.

Frequent: To go somewhere often. Sharks tend to frequent places where there are lots of fish.

Ft.: An abbreviation for feet or foot, which is a unit of measurement. It is equal to 12 inches or about .3 meters.

Indigenous: Native to a place or region.

Intimidate: To scare or cause fear. Sharks can intimidate other fish and humans because of their fierce teeth.

Invincible: Unable to be beaten or killed. Sharks seem to be invincible, but some species are endangered.

KPH: An abbreviation for kilometers per hour, which is a metric unit of measurement for speed. One kilometer is equal to approximately .62 miles.

M: An abbreviation for meters, which is a metric unit of measurement for distance. One meter is equal to approximately 3.28 feet.

Mi.: An abbreviation for miles, which is a unit of measurement for distance. One mile is equal to approximately 1.61 kilometers.

Migrate: To move from one place to another. Sharks often migrate from cool to warm water for several different reasons.

MPH: An abbreviation for miles per hour, which is a unit of measurement for speed. One mile is equal to approximately 1.61 kilometers.

Phenomenon: Something that is unusual or amazing. Seeing sharks in the wild can be quite a phenomenon.

Prey: Animals that are hunted for food—either by humans or other animals. It can also mean the act of hunting.

Reputable: Something that is considered to be good or to have a good reputation. When diving with sharks, it is important to find a reputable company that has been in business for a long time.

Staple: Something that is important in a diet. Vegetables are staples in our diet, and fish is a staple in sharks' diets.

Strategy: A plan or method for achieving a goal. Different shark species have different hunting strategies.

Temperate: Something that is not too extreme such as water temperature. Temperate waters are not too cold or too hot.

Tentacles: Long arms on an animal that are used to move or sense objects. Octopi have tentacles that help them catch food.

Vulnerable: Something that is easily attacked. We don't think of sharks as being vulnerable, but they are when they're being hunted by humans.

INDEX

FURTHER READING

Bolster, Rob and Jerry Pallotta. *Hammerhead vs. Bull Shark: Who Would Win?* New York City: Scholastic. 2016.

Hopper, Whitney. *In Search of Bull Sharks*. PowerKids Press. 2016.

Niver, Heather Moore. *Animals of the Night: Bull Sharks After Dark*. Berkeley Heights: Ensley Publishing. 2016.

Owings, Lisa. *Animal Attacks: Bull Shark Attack*. North Mankato: Bellweather Media, Inc. 2013.

Rake, Jody Sullivan. *Bull Shark*. Mankato: Capstone Press. 2011. New York: PowerKids Press. 2016.

INTERNET RESOURCES

http://cnso.nova.edu: The Halmos College of Natural Sciences and Oceanography provides shark videos and shark activity maps.

http://cnso.nova.edu/sharktracking: The Guy Harvey Research Institute (GHRI) Shark Tracking partners with the Halmos College of Natural Sciences and Oceanography in tracking and recording shark activity. The GHRI dedicates its resources to the preservation of marine life, including sharks.

http://discoverykids.com/category/sharks/: The Discovery Kids site provides shark games, videos, activities, facts, and stories.

https://www.discovery.com/tv-shows/shark-week/: The Discovery Channel's Shark Week provides information on a variety of species of sharks. Their website provides videos, shark facts, and diagrams to help you learn more about sharks.

https://kids.nationalgeographic.com/explore/youtube-playlist-pages/youtube-playlist-sharks/: The National Geographic Kids' YouTube playlist provides over three hundred hours of exciting shark videos selected by kids.

http://www.ocearch.org/#Home: Ocearch provides an interactive map that allows you to track tagged sharks in real time.

http://saveourseas.com: The Save Our Seas Foundation focuses their efforts specifically on saving sharks and rays. Their website includes shark facts, a newsletter, and details about how to help save sharks and rays.

http://www.seafoodwatch.org/: Seafood Watch helps educate consumers about the fishing practices of commercial fisheries. It's a good idea to check this site before you purchase seafood to see if the company you are purchasing from engages in sustainable fishing practices.

AT A GLANCE

Source: www.iucnredlist.org

SWIM DEPTH

- 200 ft.
- 400 ft.
- 600 ft.
- 800 ft.
- 1,000 ft.
- 1,200 ft.
- 1,400 ft.
- 1,600 ft.
- 1,800 ft.

Hammerhead Sharks
Length: 20 ft. (6.1 m)
Swim Depth: 262 ft. (80 m)
Lifespan: 20+ years

Bull Sharks
Length: 11.1 ft. (3.4 m)
Swim Depth: 492 ft. (150 m)
Lifespan: 18+ years

Rays
Length: 8.2 ft. (2.5 m)
Swim Depth: 656 ft. (200 m)
Lifespan: 30 years

Great White Sharks
Length: 19.6 ft. (6 m)
Swim Depth: 820 ft. (250 m)
Lifespan: 30 years

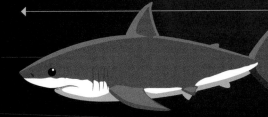

Blue Sharks
Length: 12.5 ft. (3.8 m)
Swim Depth: 1,148 ft. (350 m)
Lifespan: 20 years

Tiger Sharks
Length: 11.5 ft. (3.5 m)
Swim Depth: 1148 ft. (350 m)
Lifespan: 50 years

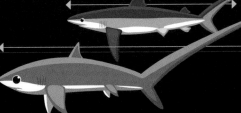

Thresher Sharks
Length: 18.7 ft. (5.7 m)
Swim Depth: 1200 ft. (366 m)
Lifespan: 50 years

Mako Sharks
Length: 13.1 ft. (4 m)
Swim Depth: 1,640 ft. (500 m)
Lifespan: 32 years

PHOTO CREDITS

EDUCATIONAL VIDEO LINKS

Chapter 1
Watch this video of researchers studying shark attacks in the Bay of Bengal.
https://www.youtube.com/watch?v=2_x8oRSVfCQ

Chapter 2a
Although not a bull shark, this video demonstrates how sharks are captured and tagged by marine biologists.
https://www.youtube.com/watch?v=AA1IgnuBHME&t=37s

Chapter 2b
Watch this video to see how some scientists are using technology to get close to sharks: https://www.youtube.com/watch?v=SlVjt-tMTAM&t=28s

Chapter 3
Check out this video to see how marine biologists are studying the hunting habits of bull sharks:
https://www.youtube.com/watch?v=Kj6hDpj95rE

Chapter 4
Watch as these divers feed hungry bull sharks by hand!
https://www.youtube.com/watch?v=vrkkQO9zVfA

AUTHOR'S BIOGRAPHY

Elizabeth Roseborough is a former college, high school, and middle school biology instructor. When not visiting her favorite Caribbean islands, Elizabeth spends her time with her husband, son, and their fur babies, Titan and Stella, at their home in Dayton, Ohio.